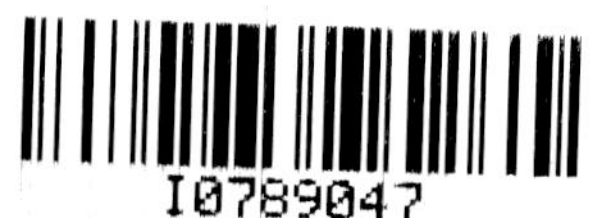

THIS COLORING BOOK
BELONGS TO:

....
....
....

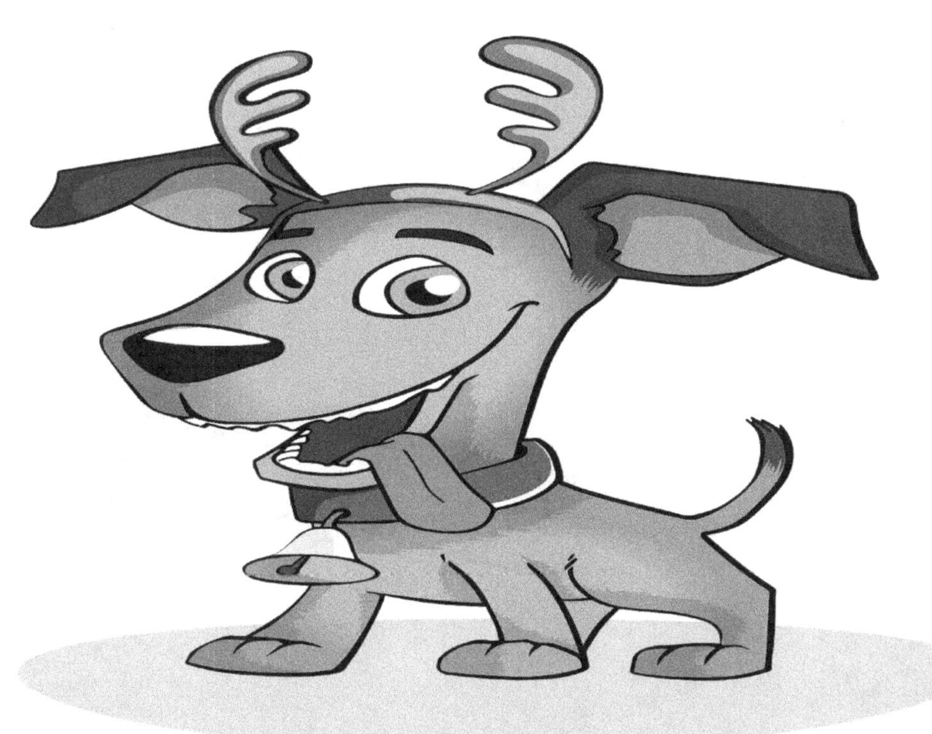

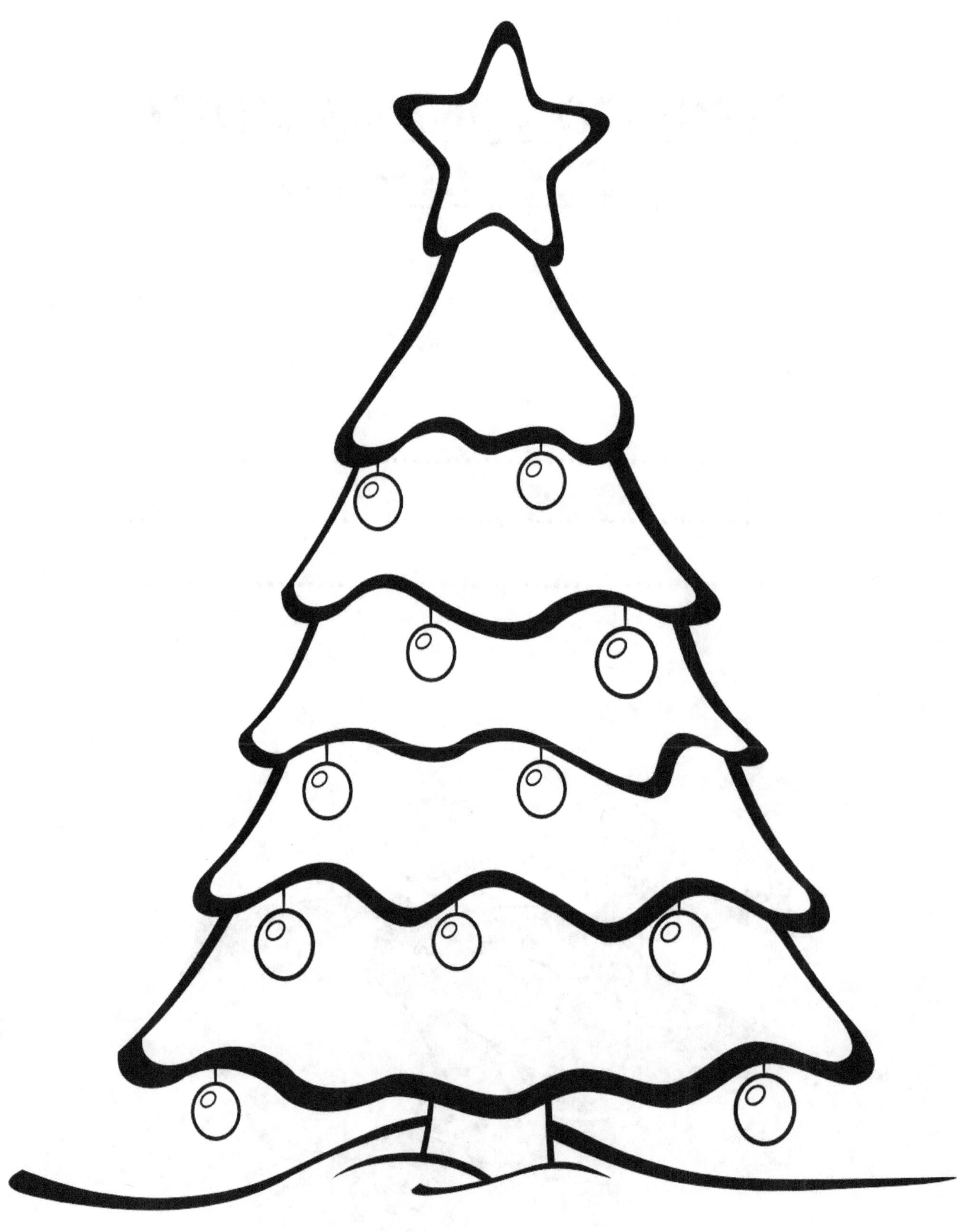

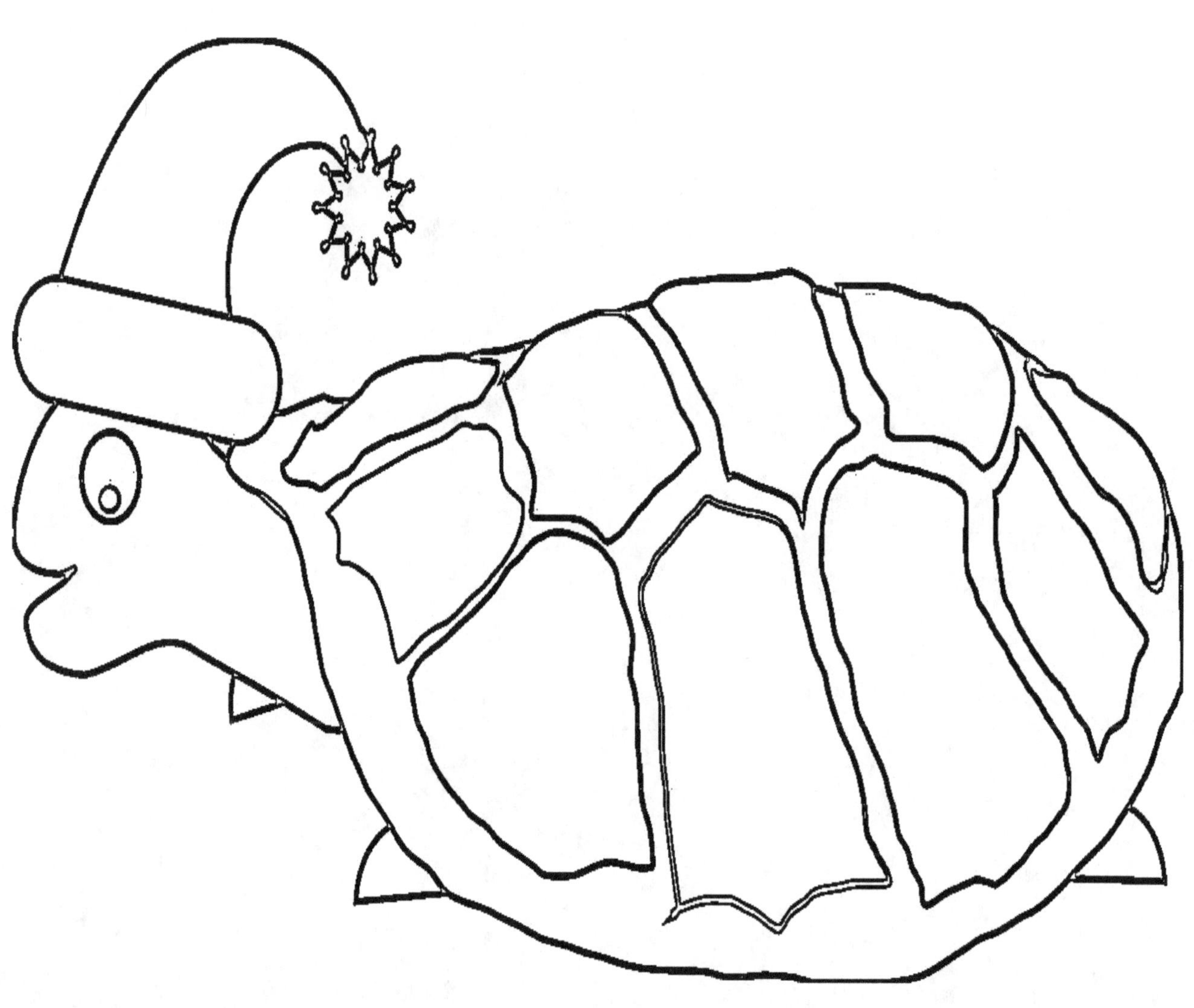

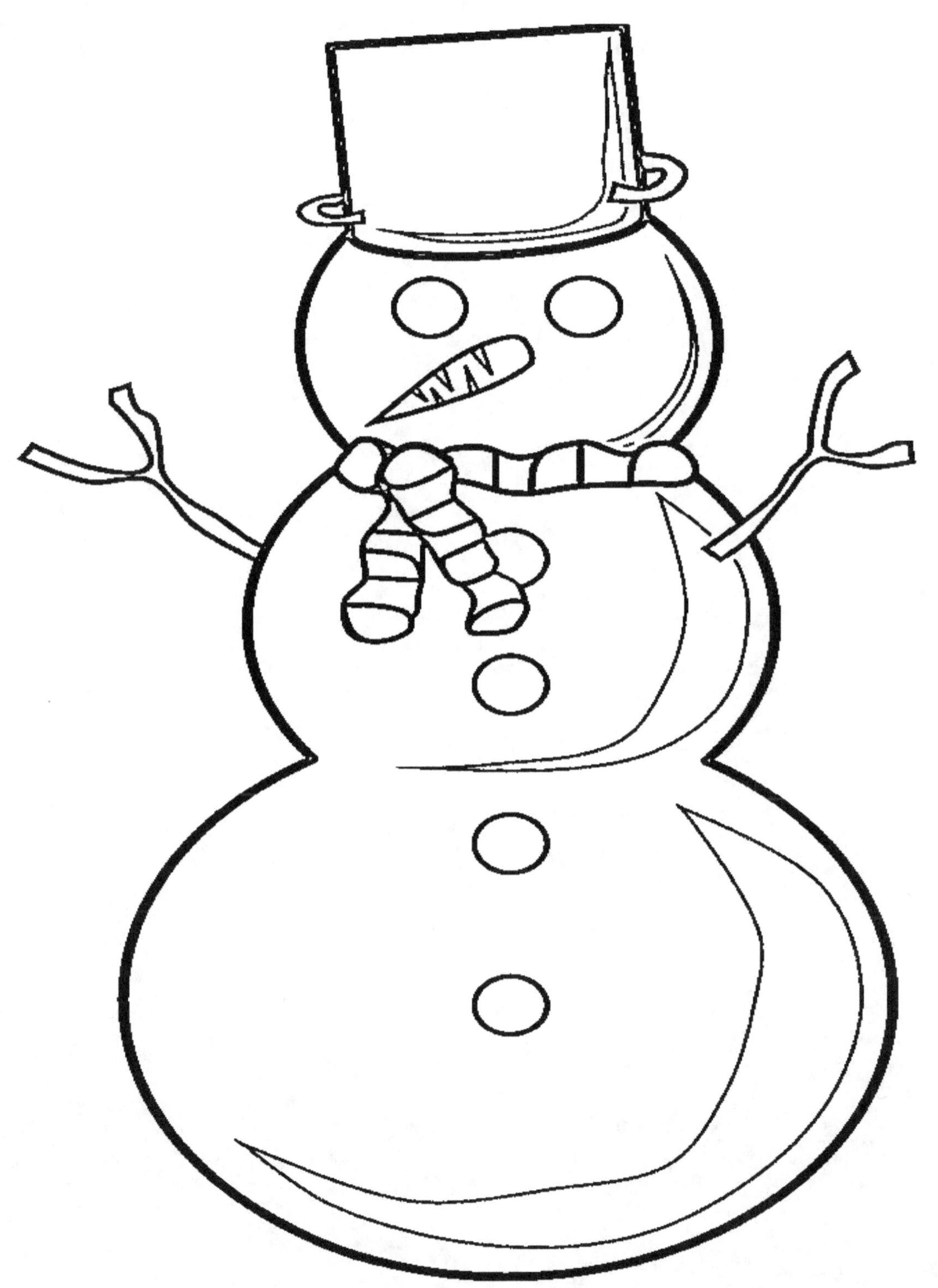

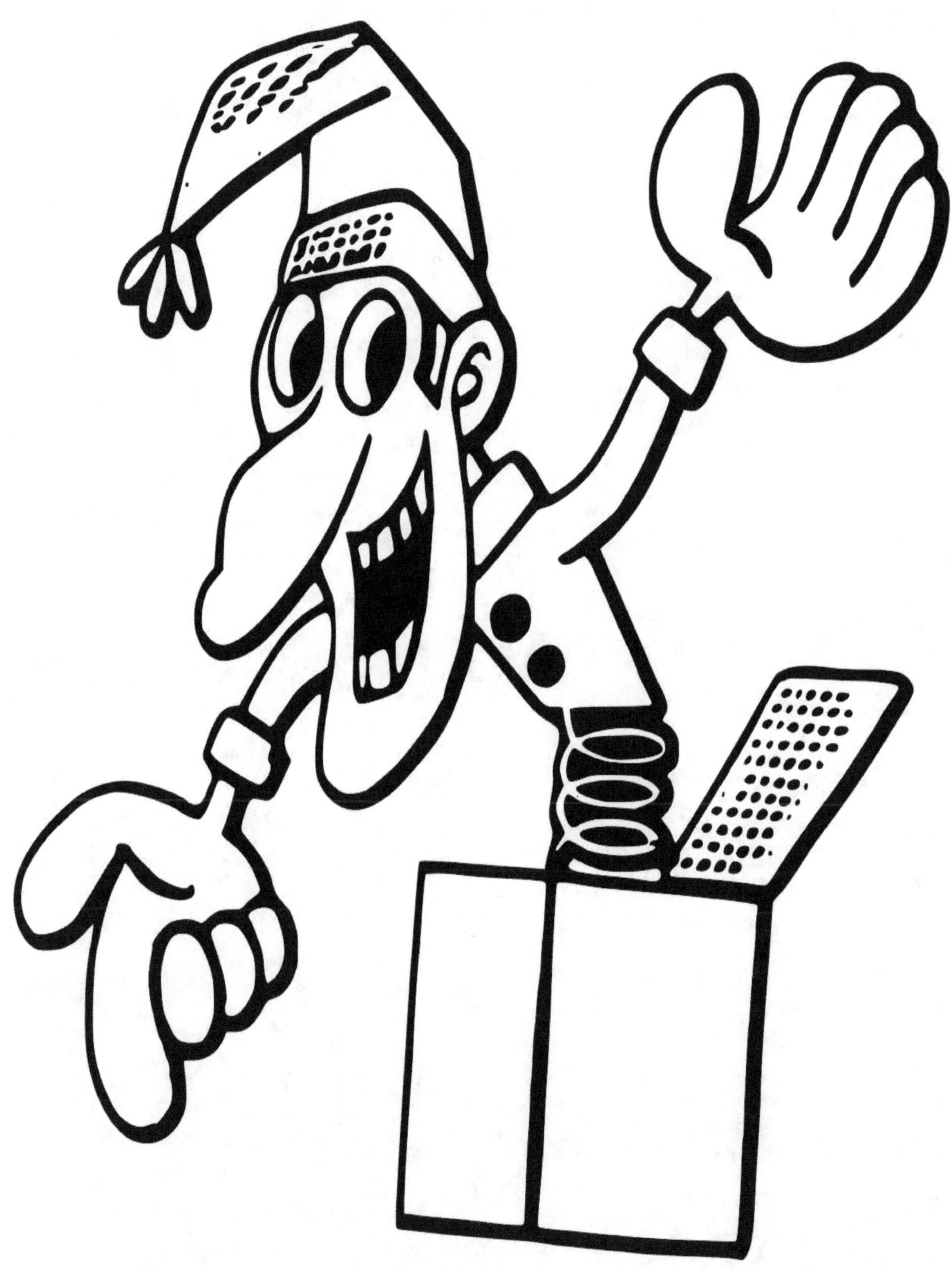

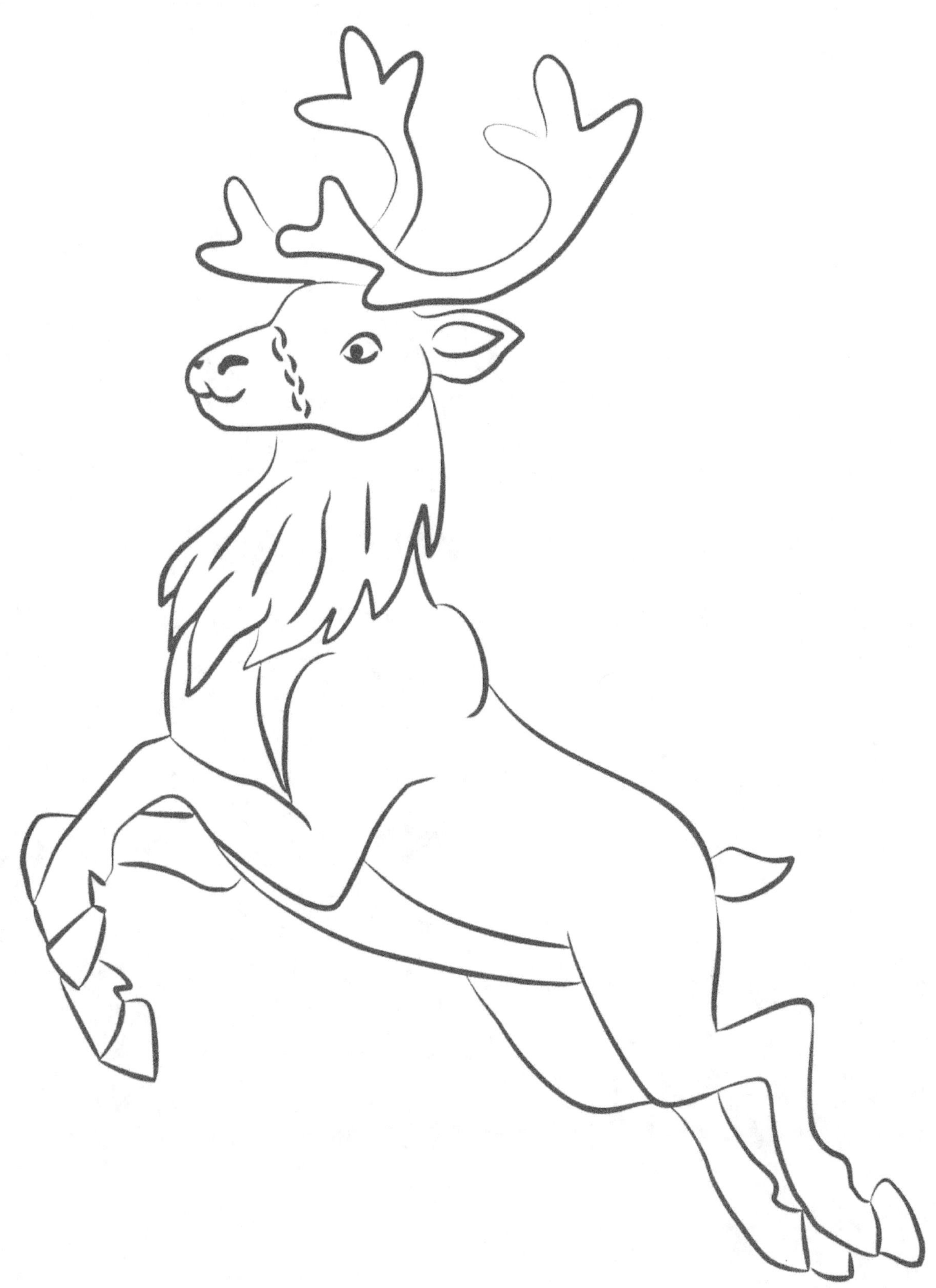

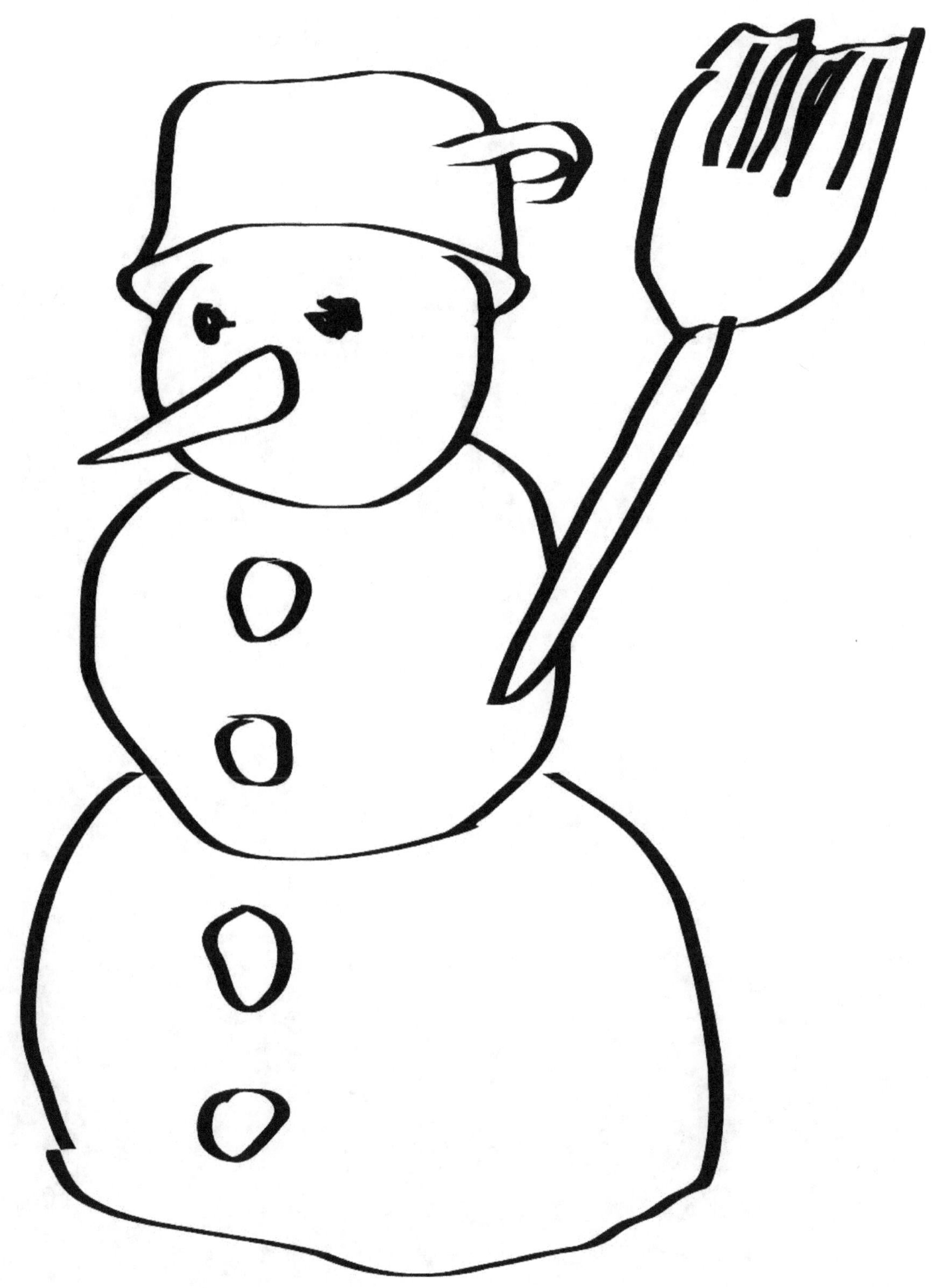

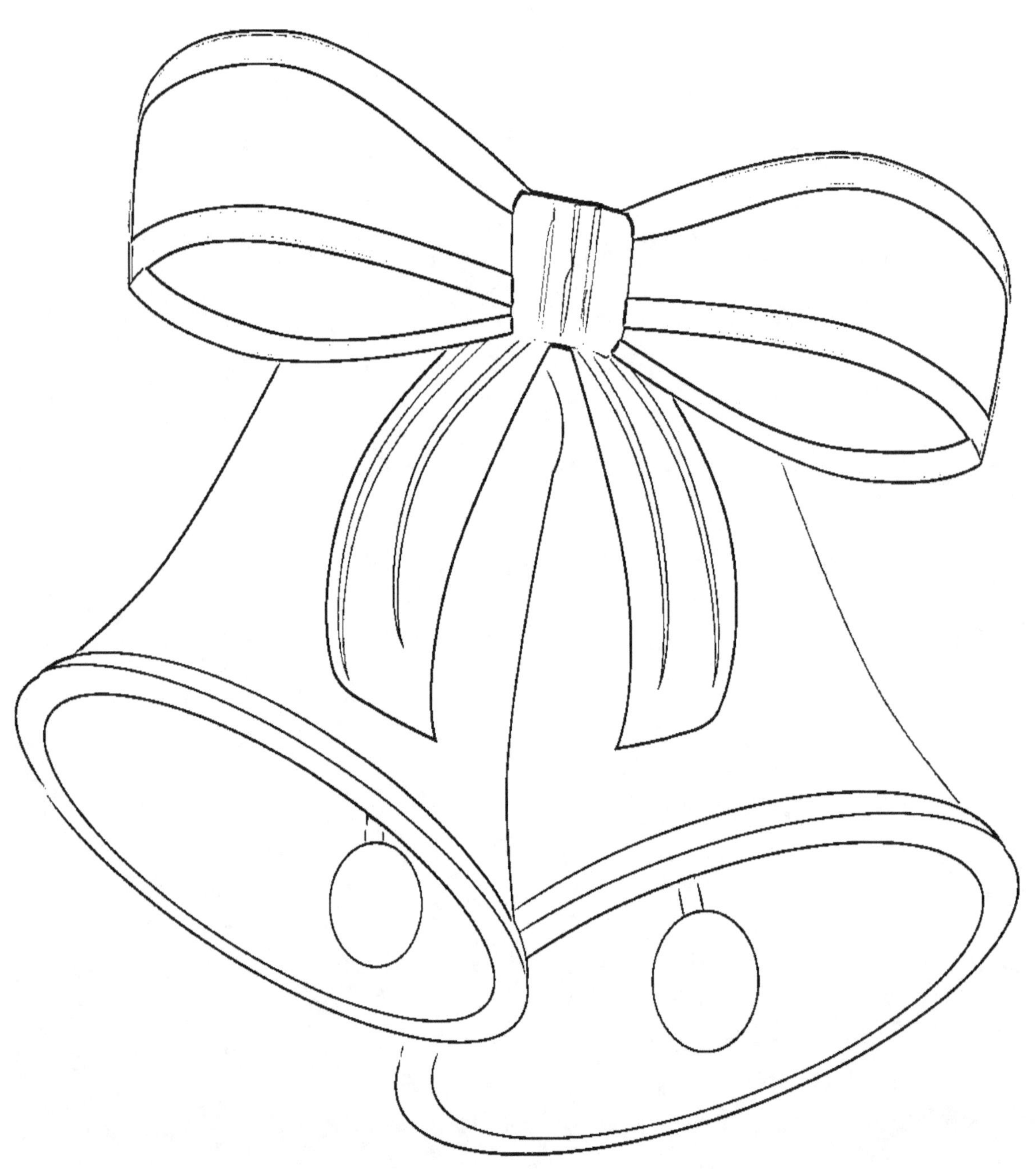

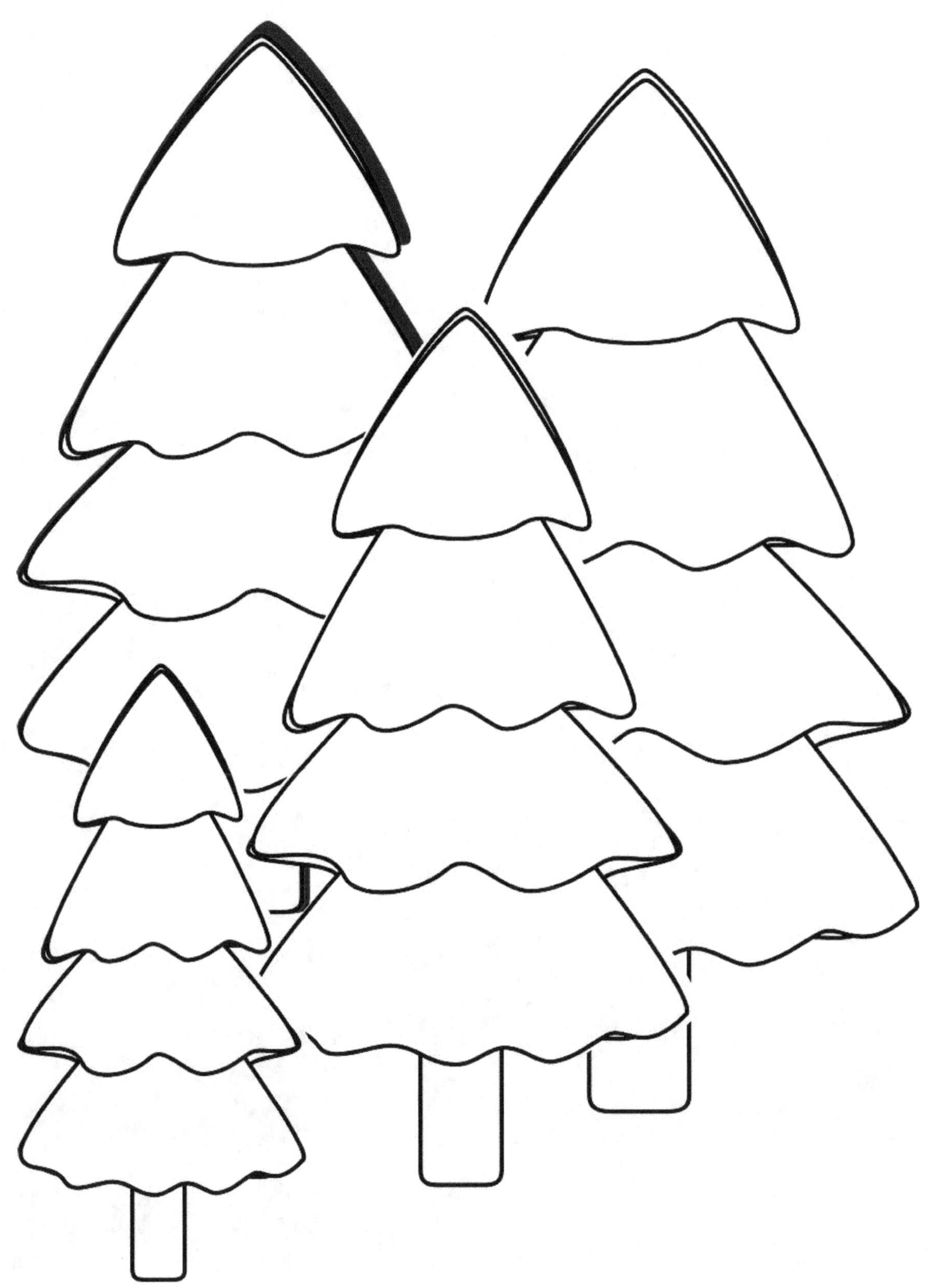

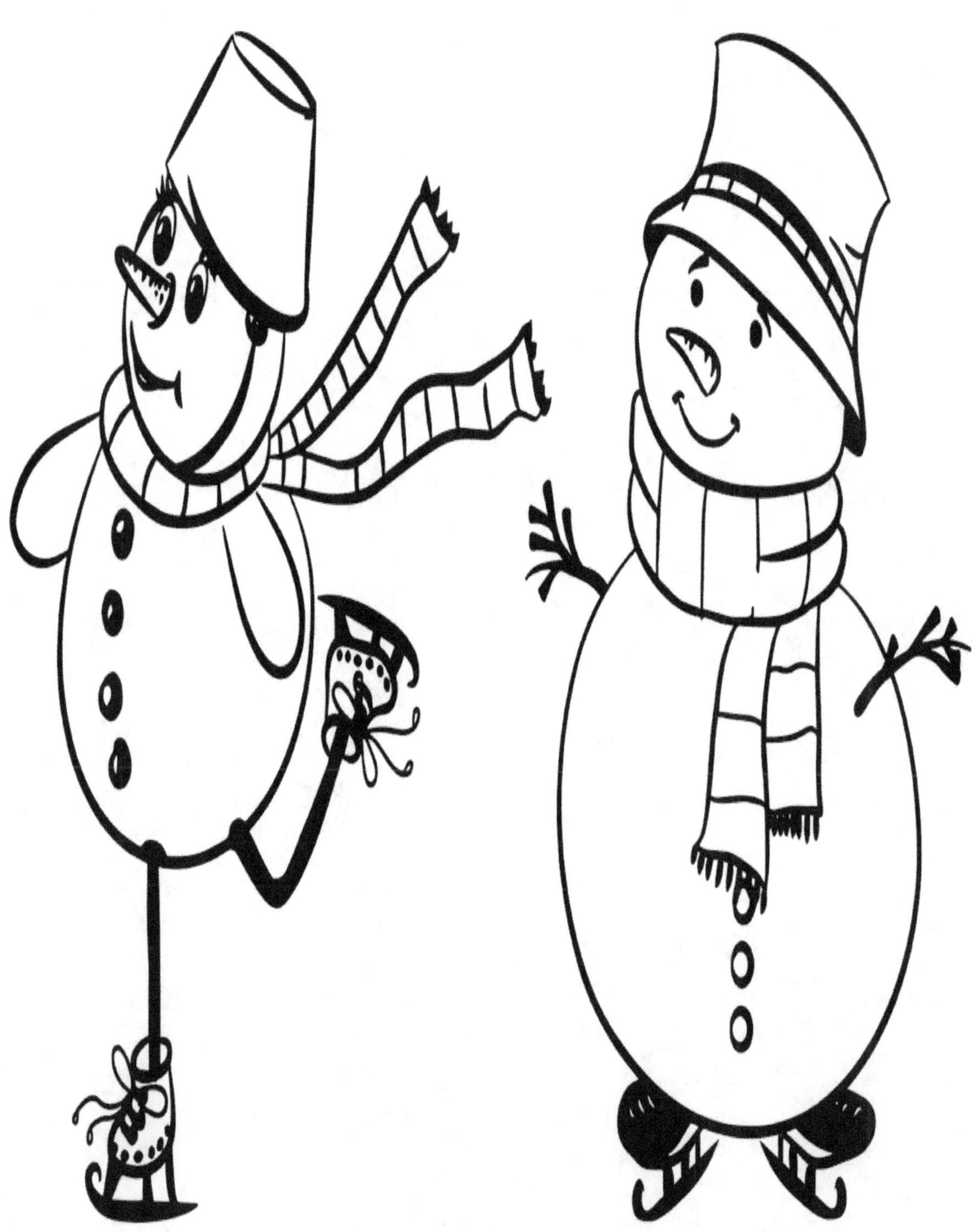

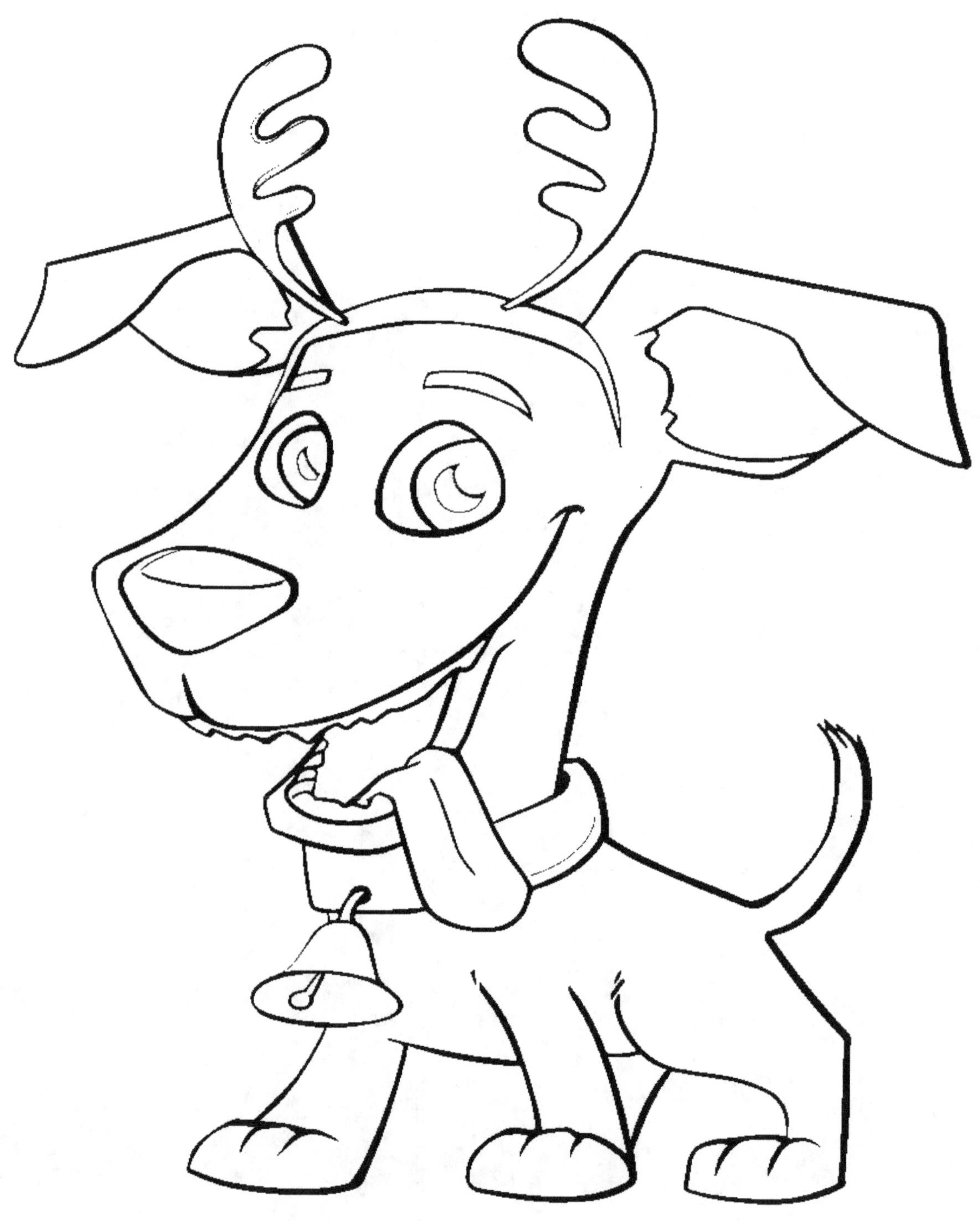

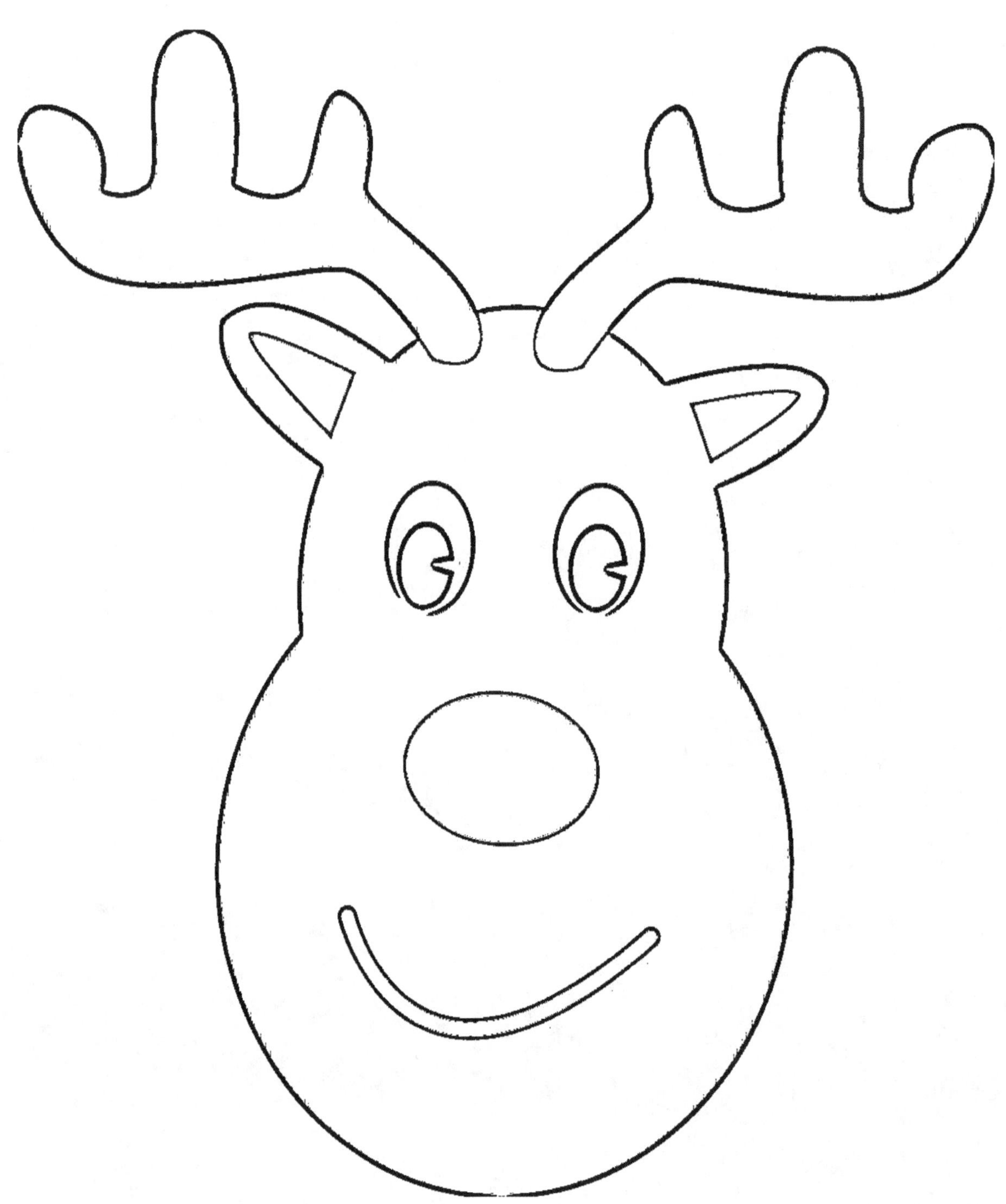

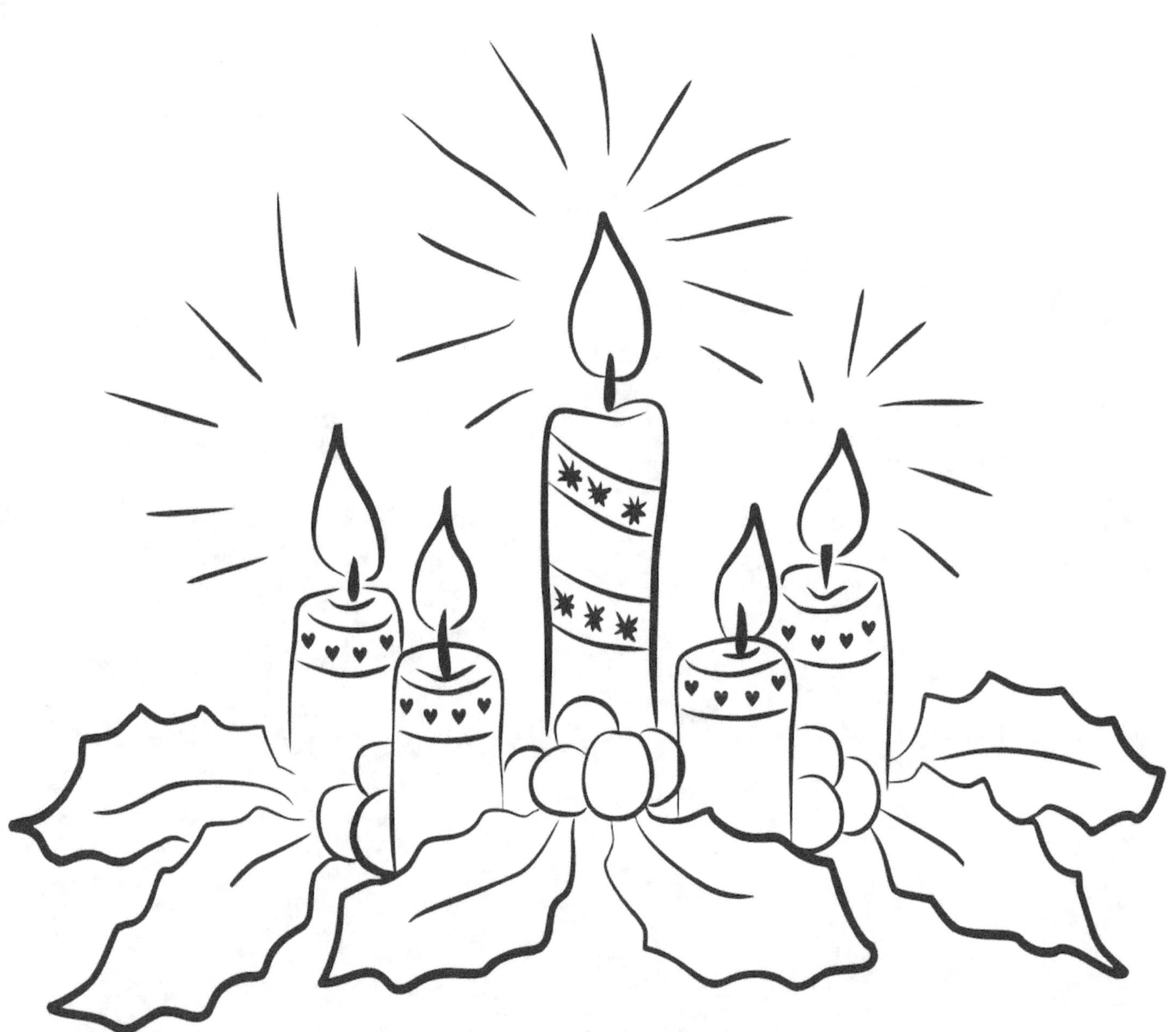

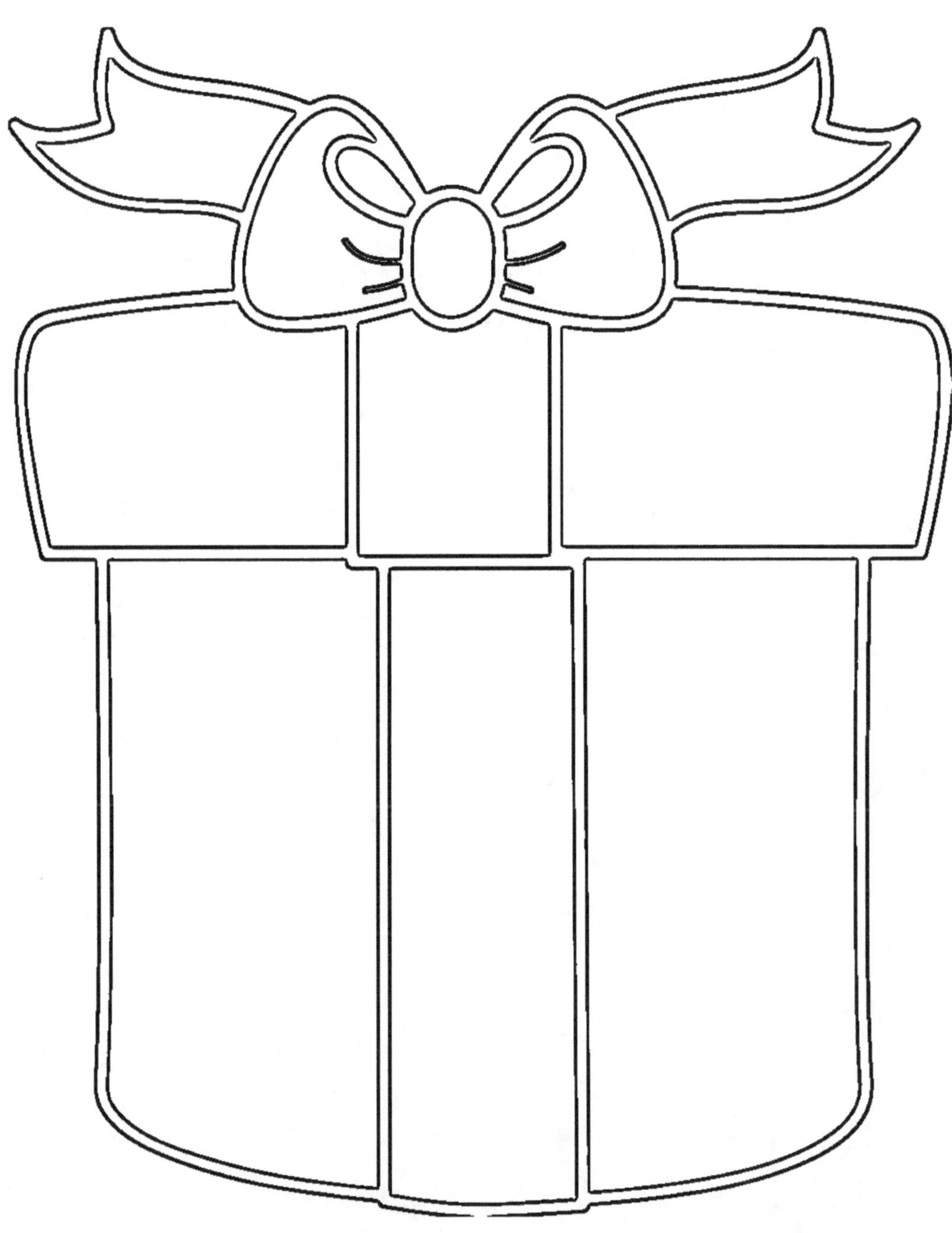

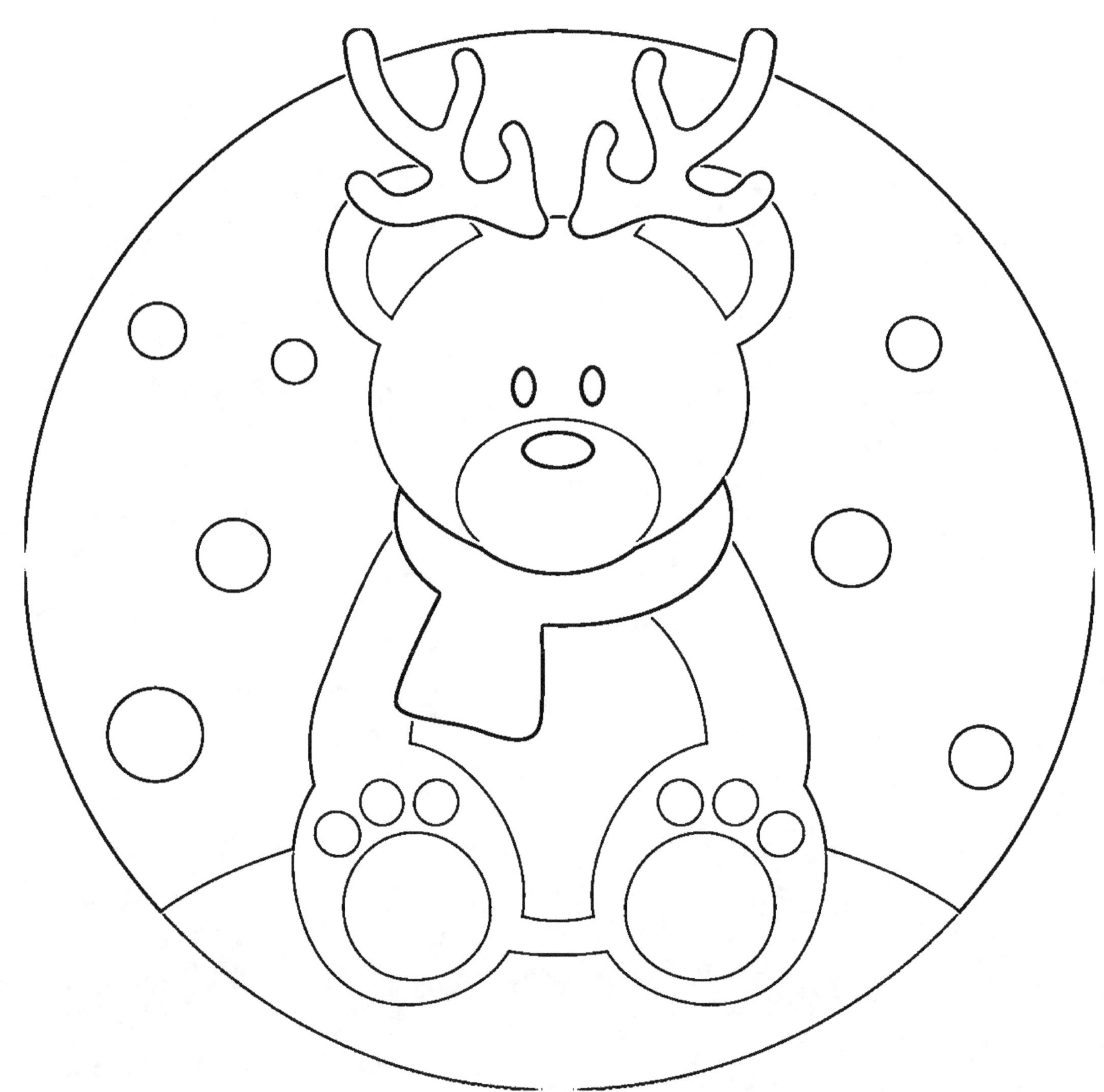

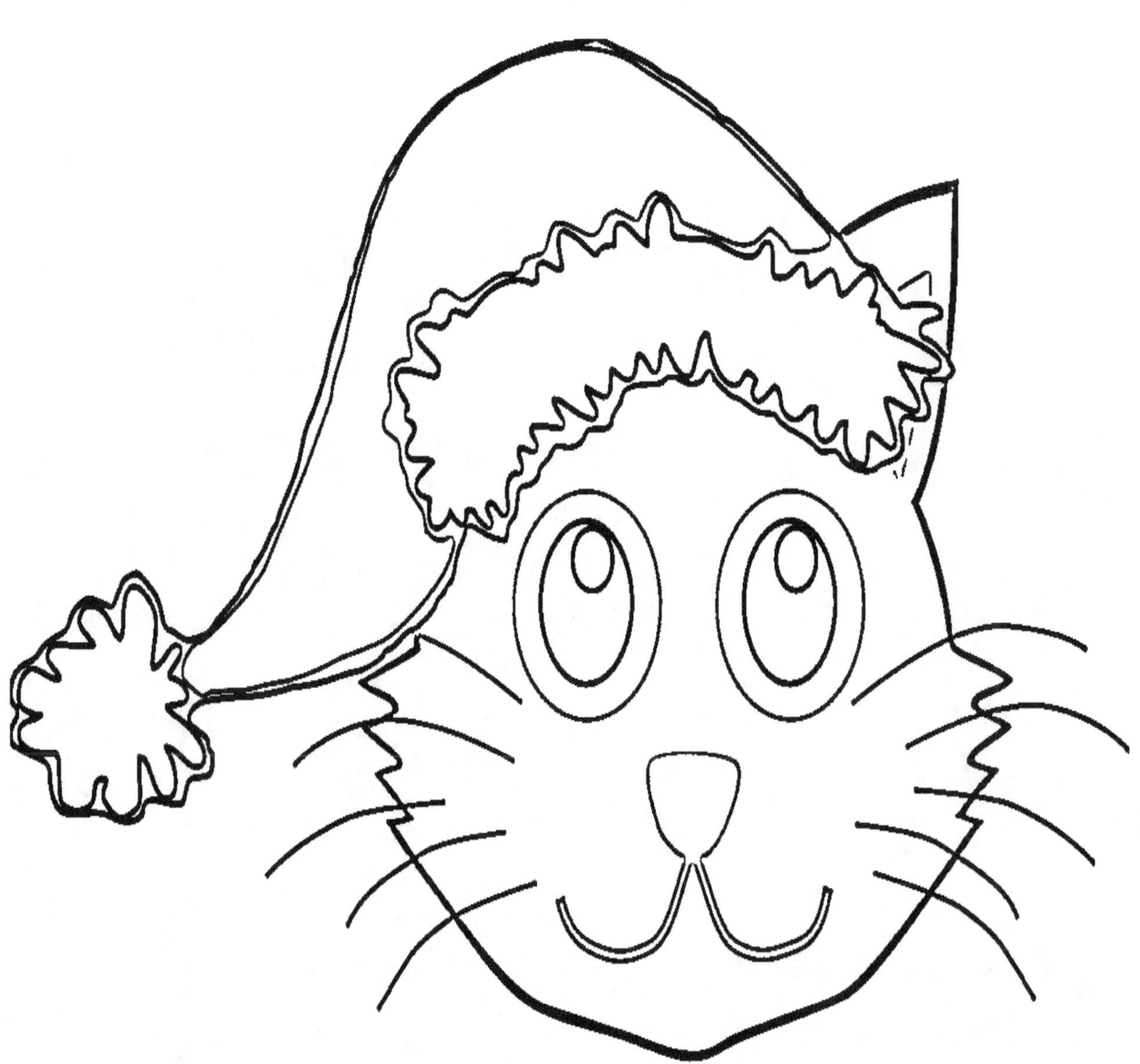

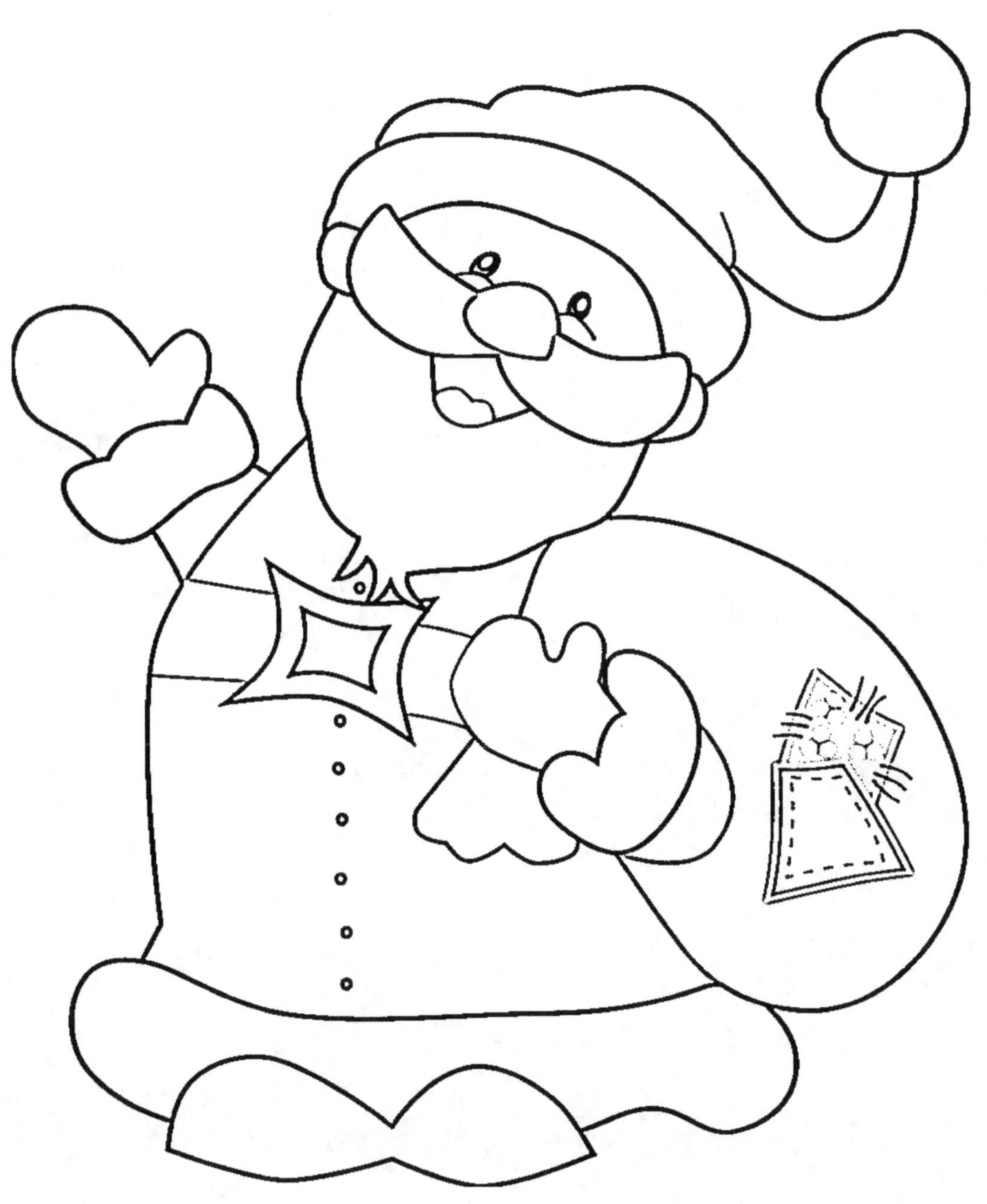

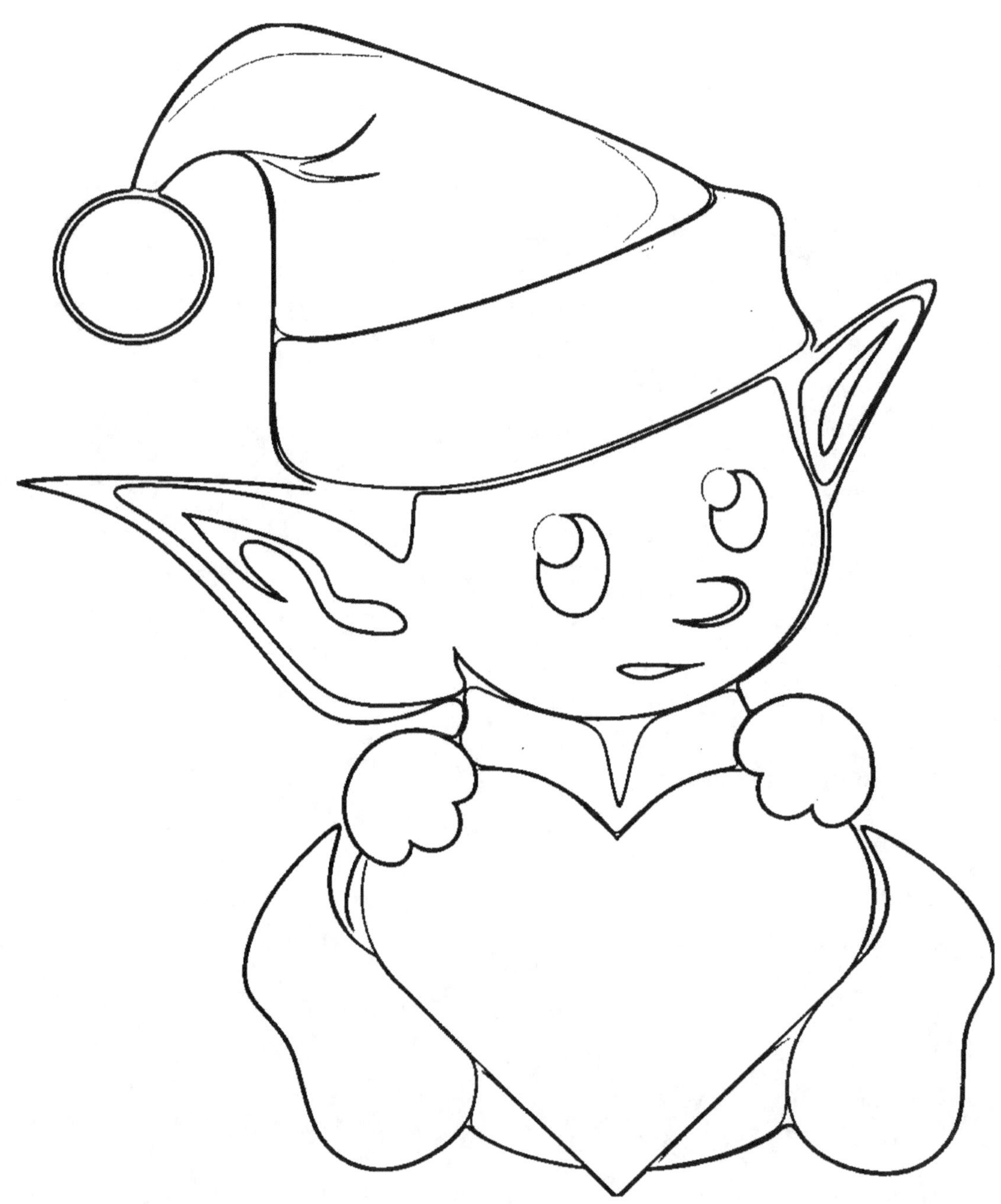

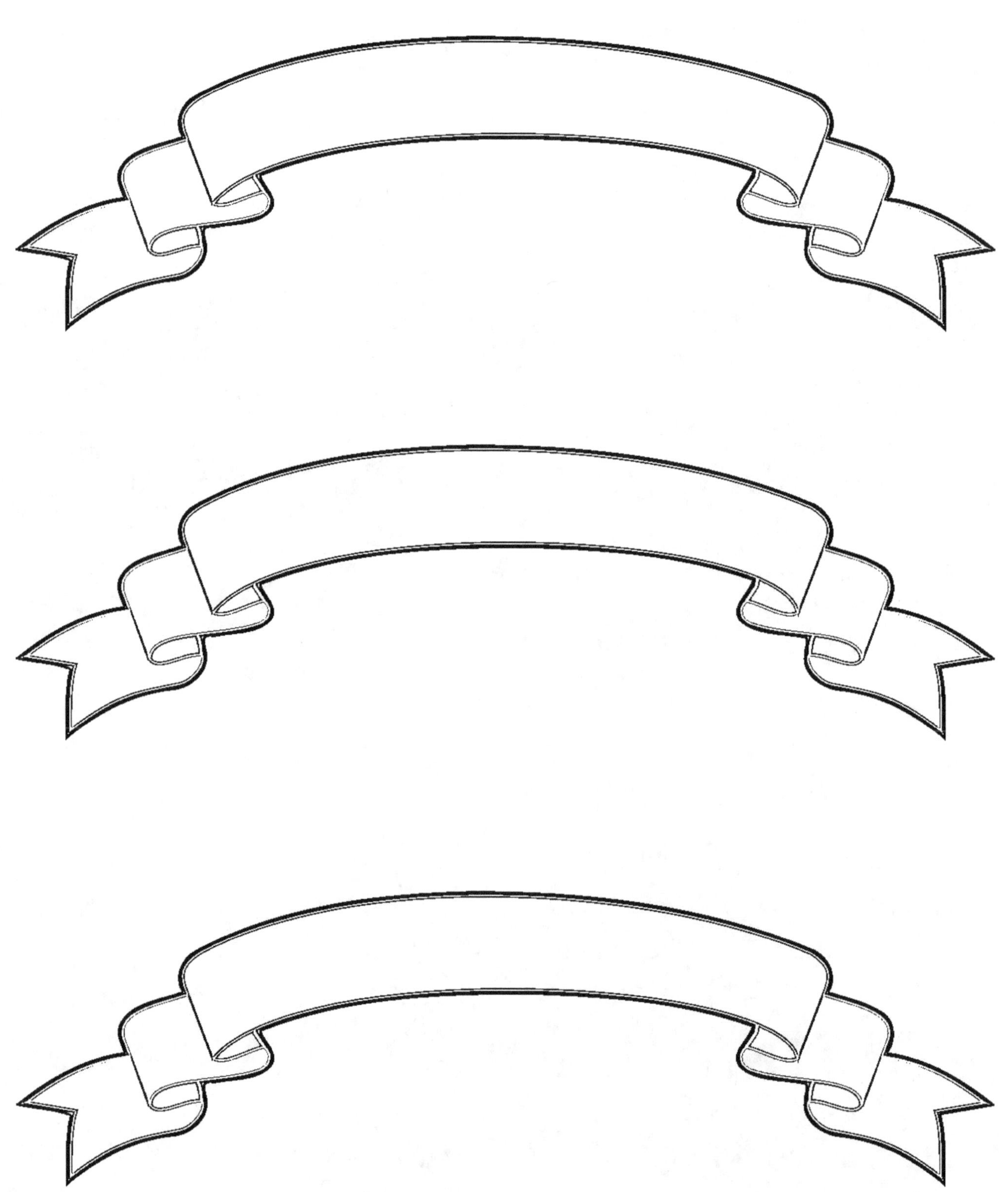

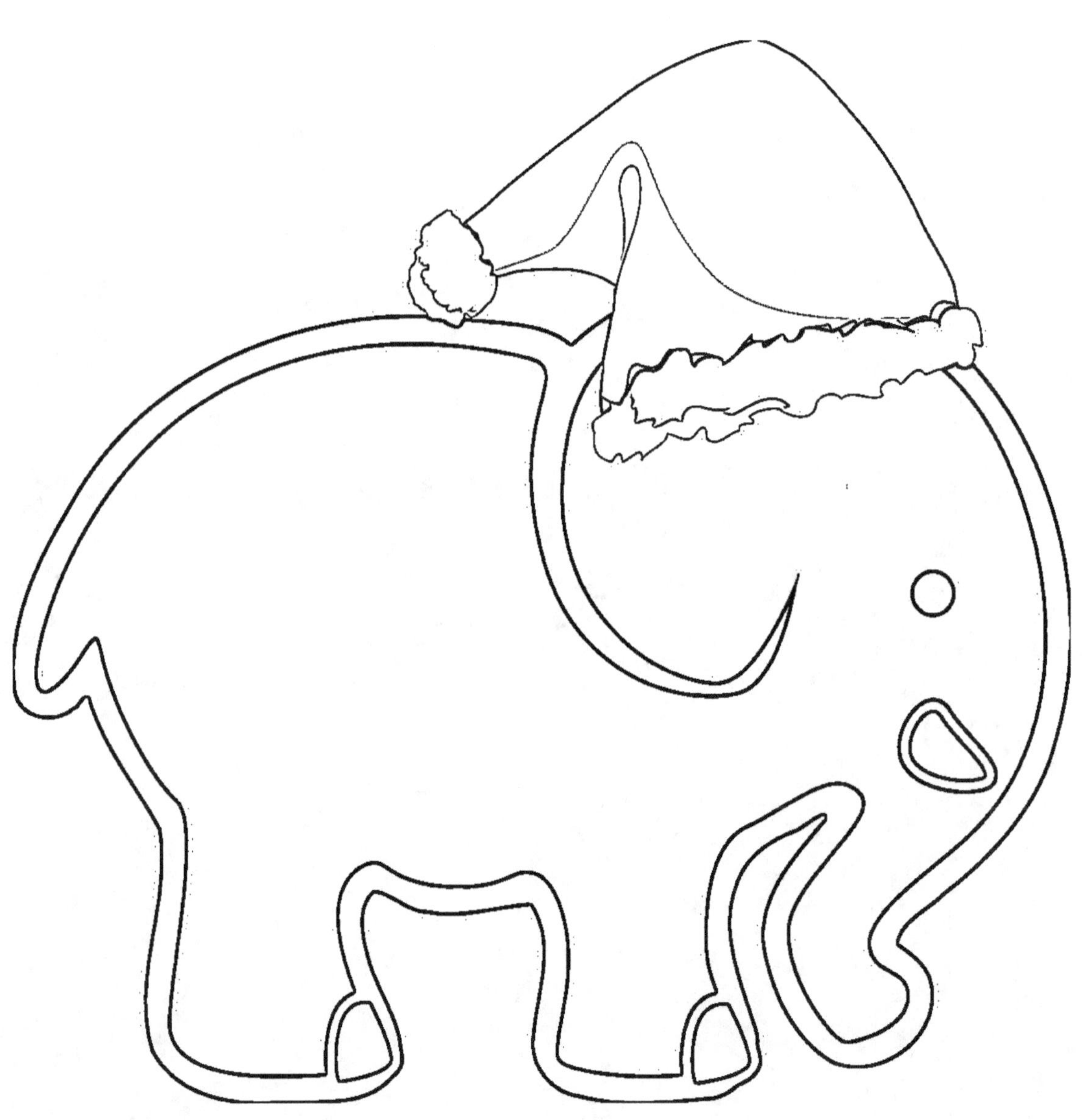

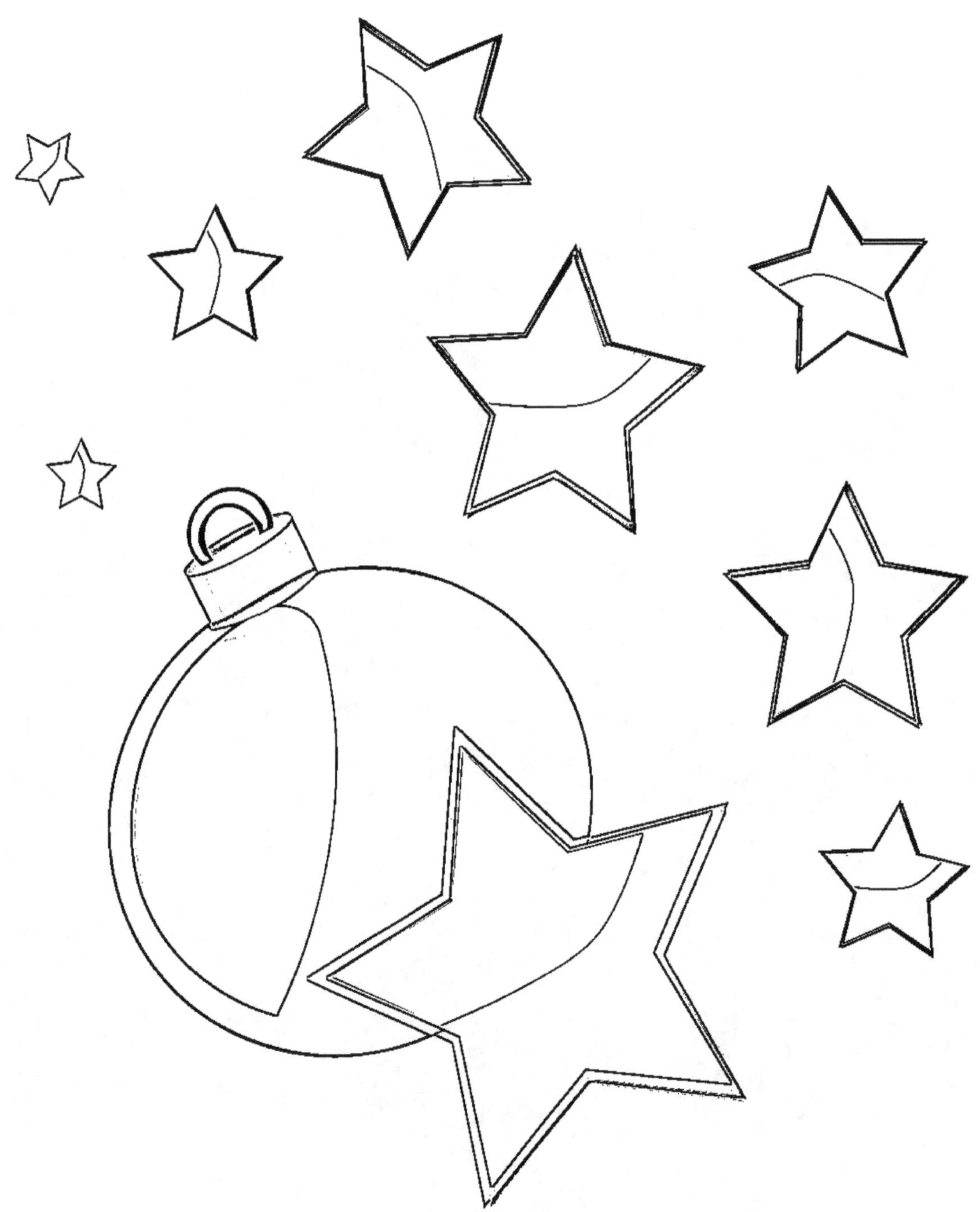

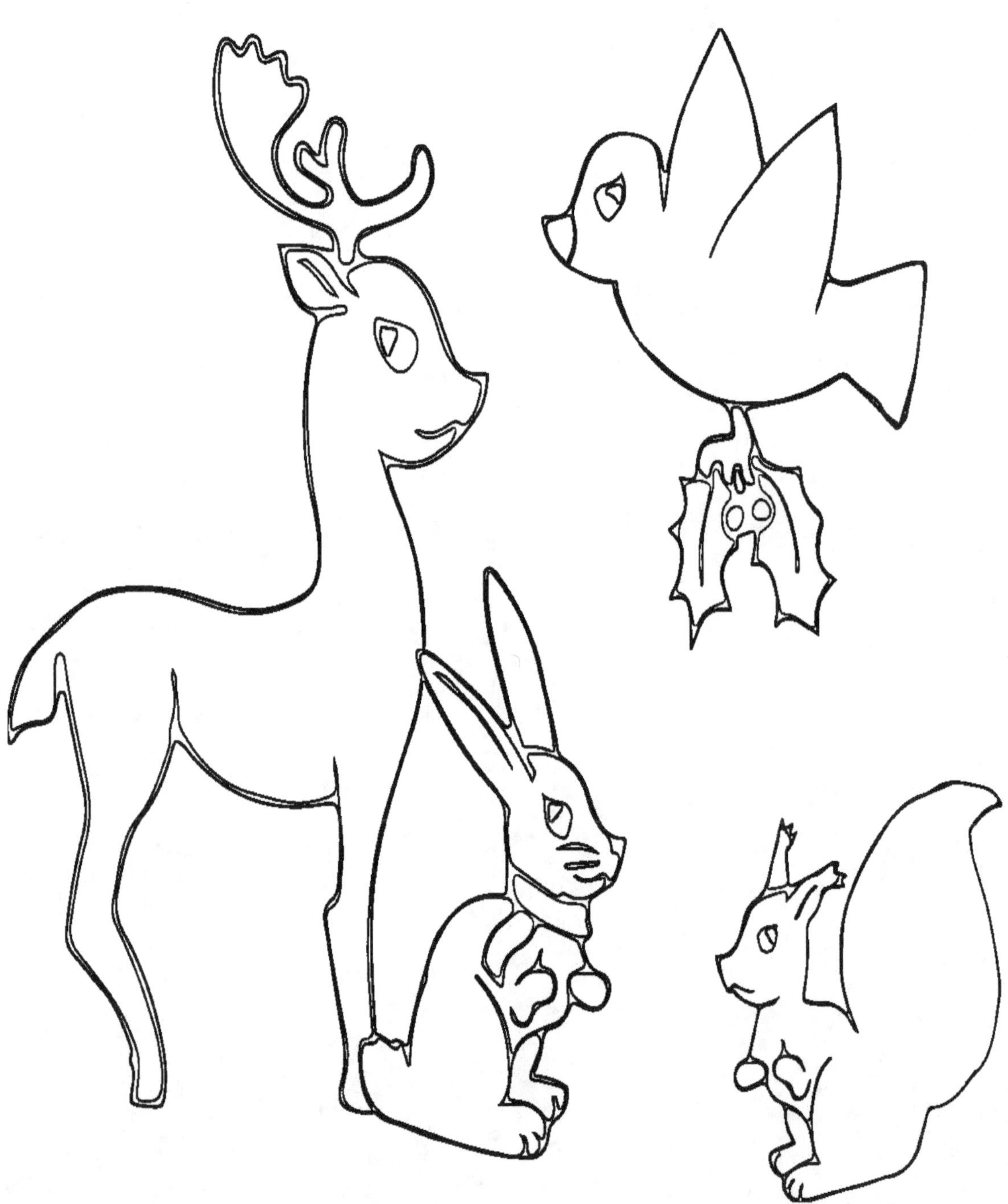

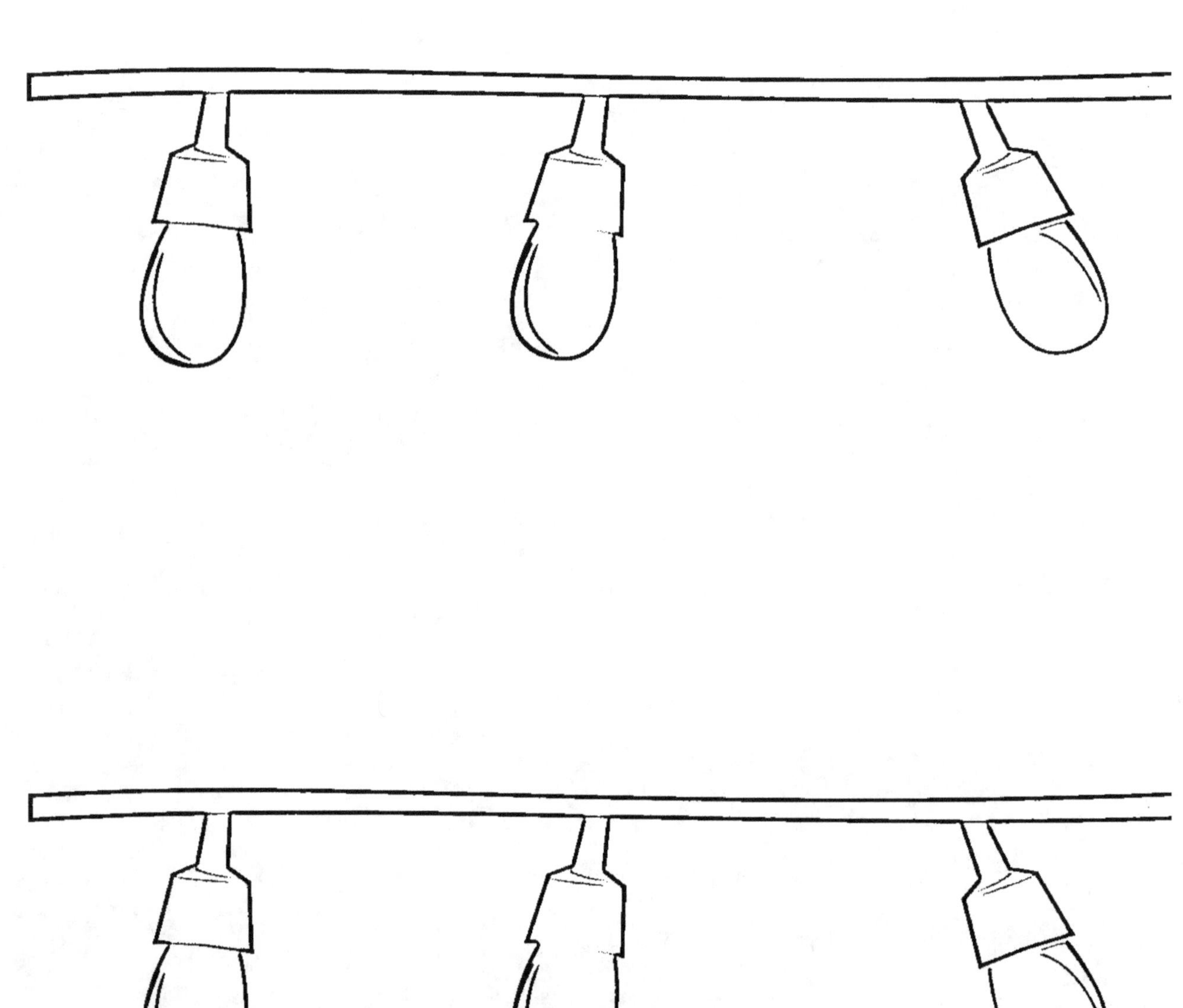

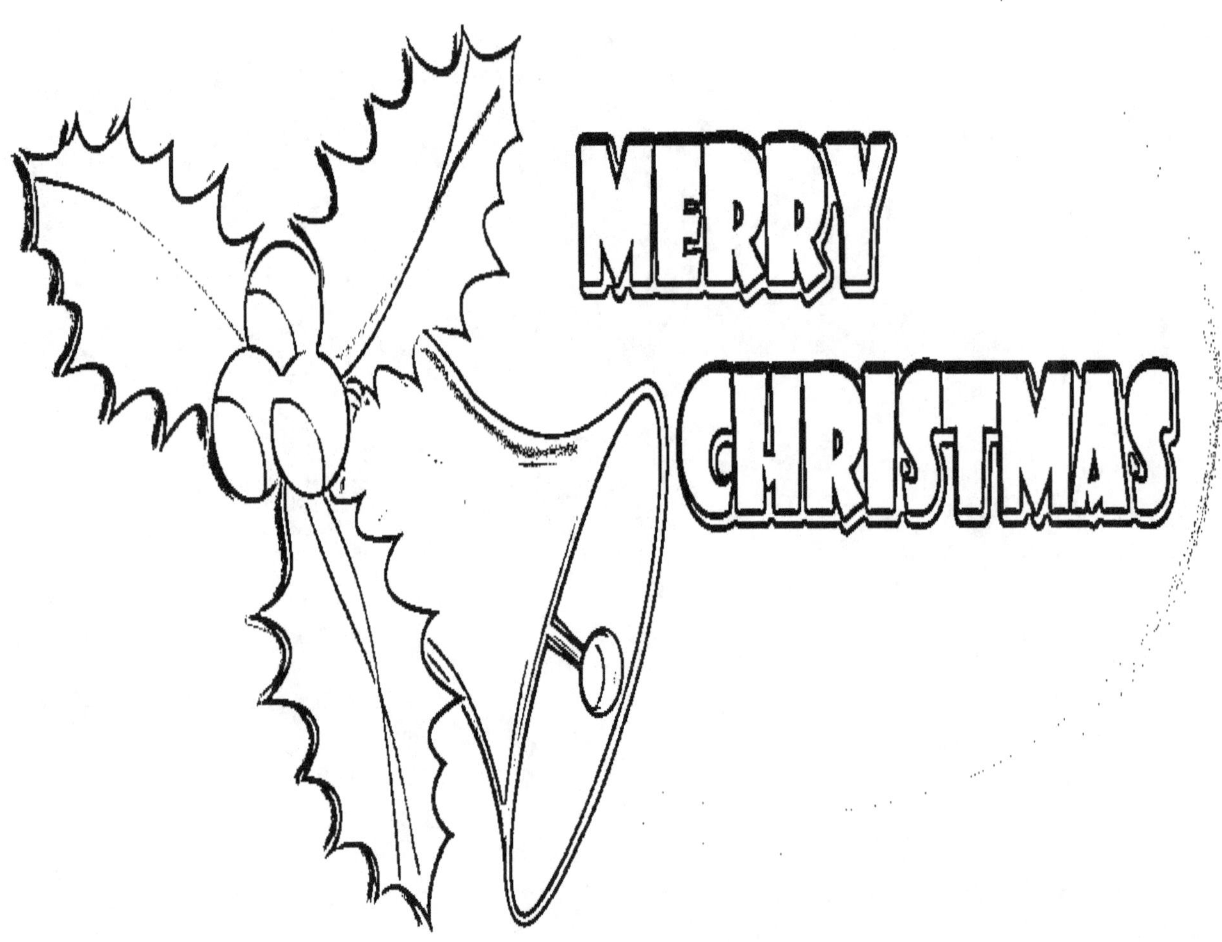

MERRY
CHRISTMAS

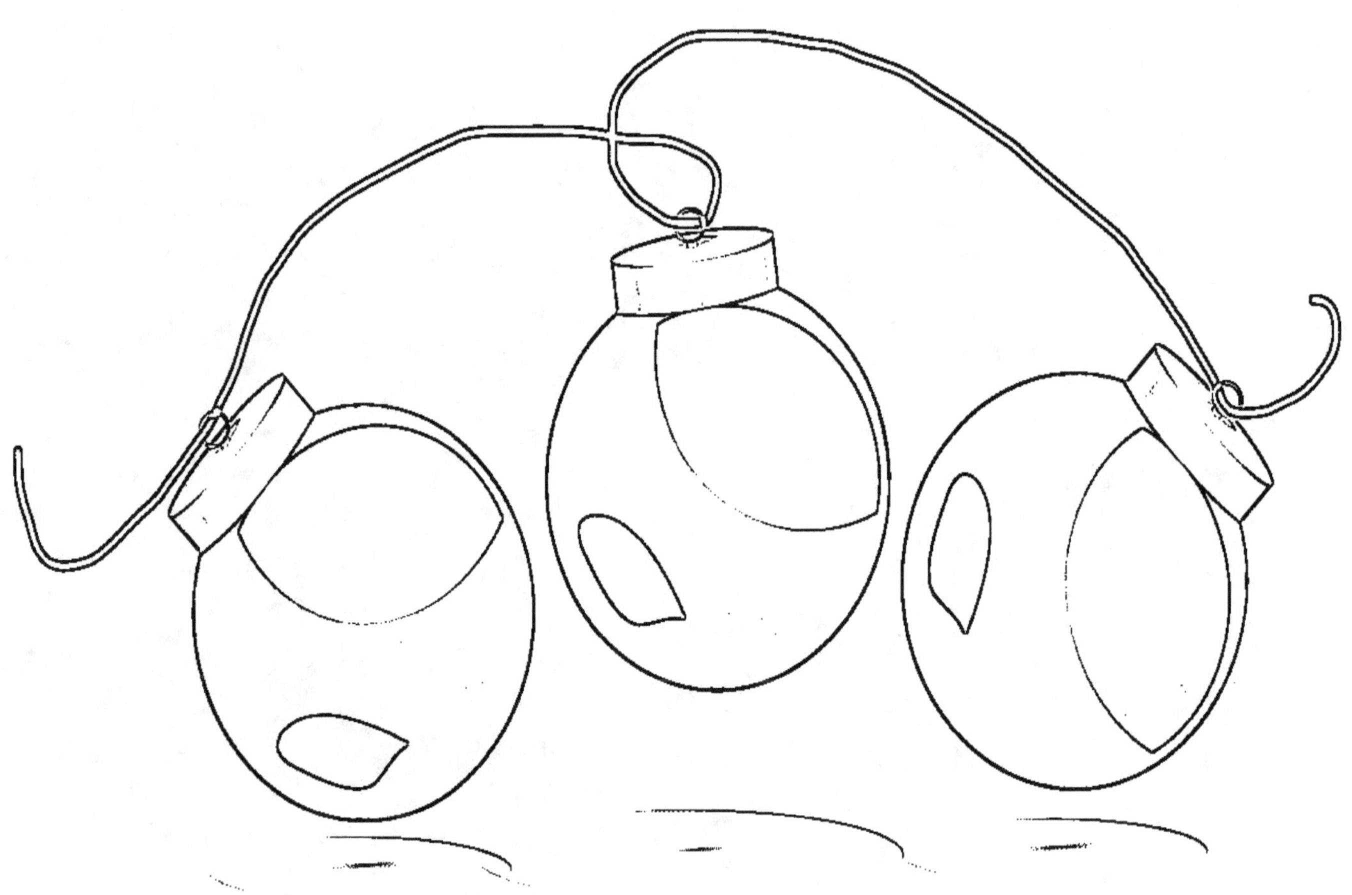

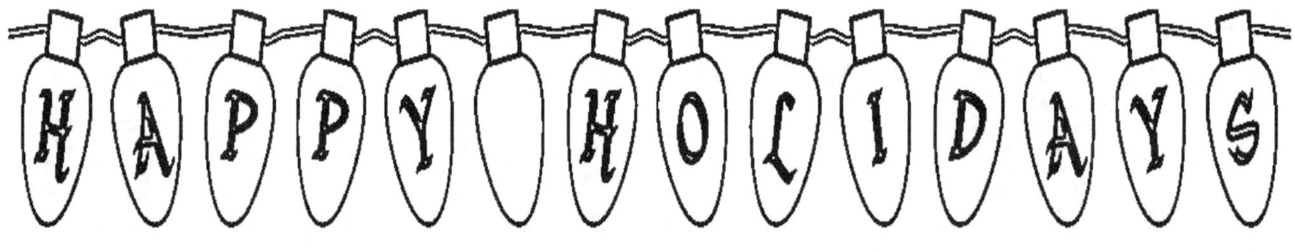

HAPPY HOLIDAYS
MERRY CHRISTMAS
HAPPY NEW YEAR